ALICE

IN WONDERLAND

LEWIS CARROLL

$\frac{f}{17703}$

Sitting around the Campfire, telling the story, were:

Wordsmith	:	Lewis Helfand
Illustrator	:	Rajesh Nagulakonda
Illustrations Editor	:	Jayshree Das
Colourist	:	KG Prasanth
Letterers	:	Bhavnath Chaudhary
		Vishal Sharma
Editors	:	Divya Dubey
		Andrew Dodd
Research Editor	:	Pushpanjali Borooah
Cover Art	:	Rajesh Nagulakonda

Published by Kalyani Navyug Media Pvt Ltd
101 C, Shiv House, Hari Nagar Ashram
New Delhi 110014
India
www.campfire.co.in

ISBN: 978-93-800280-0-2

Printed in India at Rave India

About The Author

Lewis Carroll was the pseudonym of Charles Lutwidge Dodgson. He was born on 27th January 1832 in the county of Cheshire, England and was the third of eleven children. His parents were Charles Dodgson and Frances Jane Lutwidge.

Carroll's father was known as a gifted mathematician, and it was a trait he passed onto his son. Carroll later excelled at mathematics and wrote extensively about the subject. In 1846, Carroll was sent to Rugby School and, following this, he went on to study at Oxford University's Christ Church in 1851. That same year his mother died from inflammation of the brain.

After obtaining his degree, Carroll remained at Christ Church to teach, but his interests branched out far beyond mathematics. He began to concentrate on writing fiction and first used the Lewis Carroll pseudonym for a poem called *Solitude* in 1856.

That same year Henry Liddell arrived at Christ Church with his wife and children to serve as the new dean. Carroll became a close friend of the family, and would entertain Liddell's children with his fantastic stories. At the insistence of Alice, one of Liddell's daughters, Carroll wrote *Alice's Adventures Underground* in 1864. This collection of stories served as the basis for *Alice's Adventures in Wonderland*, which was published one year later.

When *Alice's Adventures in Wonderland* became an overwhelming success, Carroll published a sequel, known as *Through the Looking Glass*, in 1872. As he continued with his writing and teaching careers, Carroll also pursued a number of other passions including art and photography. He is also credited with inventing a word game known as *Doublets*.

Lewis Carroll passed away on 14th January 1898 at the age of 65.

ALICE

WHITE RABBIT

MAD HATTER

KING

QUEEN

Alice was not hurt at all. Before her was another long passage, and the White Rabbit was still in sight, hurrying down it.

Oh my ears and whiskers, how late it's getting!

Suddenly, the Rabbit was nowhere to be seen. There were doors all round the hall, but they were all locked.

Trying every door, Alice walked sadly down the hall, wondering how she was ever going to get out again.

There's a key on that glass table.

Maybe it will help.

Alice's first idea was that the tiny golden key might belong to one of the doors of the hall, but...

...either the locks were too large, or the key was too small.

However, on the second time round, she came upon something she had not noticed before.

The door behind the curtain was about fifteen inches high.

It fits!

Alice was delighted. She opened the door and found that it led into a small passage, not much larger than a rat hole.

At the other end of the passage...

Alice had no idea what to do. Then she found a box of sweets in her pocket and handed them round as prizes.

You promised to tell me your history, you know. And why it is you hate C and D.

Mine is a long and sad tale.

It is a long tail, certainly, but why do you call it sad?

You insult me by talking such nonsense!

You're so easily offended, you know! Please come back and finish your story!

Ah, my dear! Let this be a lesson to you never to lose your temper!

I wish I had our Dinah here, I do! She'd soon fetch it back!

And who is Dinah, if I might venture to ask the question?

Dinah's our cat. And she's so good at catching mice, you wouldn't believe it!

And oh, I wish you could see her chasing after the birds! Why, she'd eat a little bird as soon as look at it!

This speech caused a remarkable sensation among the party.

I really must be getting home; the night air doesn't suit my throat!

Come away, my dears! It's high time you were all in bed!

On various pretexts they all moved off, and Alice was soon left alone.

I wish I hadn't mentioned Dinah!

Nobody seems to like her down here, and I'm sure she's the best cat in the world. Oh, my dear Dinah! I wonder if I will see you again!

And poor Alice began to cry again, for she felt very lonely and low-spirited.

TAP TAP TAP

In a while, she heard a little pattering of footsteps in the distance, and looked up eagerly...

...half hoping that the Mouse had changed his mind, and was coming back to finish his story.

The Duchess! The Duchess! Oh my dear paws! Oh my fur and whiskers!

She'll get me executed, as sure as ferrets are ferrets! Where can I have dropped them, I wonder!

Alice guessed that the Rabbit was looking for the fan and the pair of white kid gloves, but they were nowhere to be seen.

She began hunting about for them, but everything seemed to have changed since her swim in the pool. The great hall with the glass table and the little door had vanished completely.

Why, Mary Ann, what are you doing out here?

The Rabbit's angry tone took Alice by surprise.

Run home this moment, and fetch me a pair of gloves and a fan! Quick, now!

He thought I was his housemaid. How surprised he'll be when he finds out who I am!

W. Rabbit

But I'd better take him his fan and gloves – that is, if I can find them.

She was so frightened that she ran off at once in the direction it pointed to, without trying to explain the mistake that it had made.

She went in without knocking, and hurri[ed] upstairs, feeling frightened in case sh[e] should be thrown out of the house.

She had found her way into a tidy little room, and was just going to leave, when her eyes fell upon a little bottle.

I do hope it'll make me grow large again, for I'm quite tired of being such a tiny little thing!

I know something interesting is sure to happen whenever I eat or drink anything. So I'll just see what this bottle does.

It did indeed, and much sooner than she had expected. She soon found her head pressing against the ceiling.

That's quite enough. I hope I won't grow any more. As it is, I can't get out of the door – I do wish I hadn't drunk quite so much!

Now I can do no more, whatever happens. What *will* become of me?

At least there's no room to grow up any more here. Shall I never get any older than I am now?

That'll be a comfort, in one way – never to be an old woman – but I'll always have lessons to learn!

Oh, I shouldn't like that!

Mary Ann!

"You are old, Father William..."

And Alice continued, reciting eight verses in all.

That is not right.

Not quite right, I'm afraid.

Some of the words have got altered.

It is wrong from beginning to end.

What size do you want to be?

I'm not particular about the size; only one doesn't like changing so often, you know.

Are you content now?

Well, I should like to be a little larger. Three inches is a wretched height to be.

It is a very good height indeed!

You'll get used to it in time.

One side will make you grow taller, and the other side will make you grow shorter.

One side of what? The other side of what?

Of the mushroom.

Alice remained looking thoughtfully at the mushroom for a minute, trying to make out which were the two sides of it...

...and as it was perfectly round, she found this a very difficult question.

And now, which is which?

She nibbled a little of the right hand bit and...

After a while, Alice remembered that she still had the pieces of mushroom in her hands.

She set to work, nibbling at one, and then at the other, until she had succeeded in bringing herself down to her usual height.

How puzzling all these changes are! I'm never sure what I'm going to be, from one minute to another!

However, I've got back to my right size. The next thing is to get into that beautiful garden.

How is that to be done, I wonder?

As she said this, she suddenly came upon an open place, with a little house in it, about four feet high.

Whoever lives there, it'll never do to come upon them this size.

It would frighten them out of their wits!

So she did not venture to go near the house till she had brought herself down to nine inches high.

The door led right into a large kitchen. The Duchess was sitting on a three-legged stool, nursing a baby.

There's certainly too much pepper in that soup!

AA-CHOO!

WAAAAAA-CHOO

DUNK!

Please, would you tell me why your cat grins like that?

It's a Cheshire cat, and that's why.

I didn't know that cats could grin. I don't know of any that do.

...the cook set to work, throwing everything within her reach at the Duchess and the baby.

Oh, please mind what you're doing!

The Duchess took no notice of them even when they hit her; and the baby was howling so much already that it was quite impossible to say whether the blows hurt it or not.

They all can, and most of them do. You don't know much, and that's a fact.

WAAAAAAA-CHOO
WAAAAAAA-CHOO
AA-CHOO

If everybody minded their own business...

Alice did not at all like the tone of this remark, and thought it would be as well to introduce some other subject, when...

She had not gone much farther before she came in sight of the house of the March Hare.

She thought it must be the right house, because the chimneys were shaped like ears and the roof was thatched with fur.

It was so large a house that she did not go nearer till she had made herself about two feet high by nibbling on the mushroom.

No room! No room!

There's plenty of room!

Have some wine.

I don't see any wine.

There isn't any.

Then it wasn't very civil of you to offer it.

It wasn't very civil of you to sit down without being invited.

I didn't know it was your table. It's laid for a great many more than three.

Your hair wants cutting.

You should learn not to make personal remarks. It's very rude.

Why is a raven like a writing desk?

Yes, that's it, it's always teatime. And we've no time to wash the things between whiles.

Then you keep moving round, I suppose?

Exactly so, as the things get used up.

But what happens when you come to the beginning again?

I want a clean cup. Let's all move one place on.

The Hatter was the only one who got any advantage from the change.

Alice rather unwillingly took the place of the March Hare. She was a good deal worse off than before.

She finally got up in great disgust, and walked off. None of the others took the least notice of her going.

It's the stupidest te party I ever w at in all my life!

How are you getting on?

I don't think they play at all fairly.

And they all quarrel so dreadfully – one can't hear oneself speak. And they don't seem to have any rules in particular.

At least, if there are, nobody follows them. And you've no idea how confusing it is that all the things are alive.

I should have croqueted the Queen's hedgehog just now, only it ran away when it saw mine coming!

How do you like the Queen?

Not at all.

She's so extremely--

--likely to win, that it's hardly worthwhile finishing the game.

Who are you talking to?

It's a friend of mine – a Cheshire Cat. Allow me to introduce it.

I don't like the look of it at all. However, it may kiss my hand if it likes.

I'd rather not.

Don't be impertinent...

...and don't look at me like that!

Well, it must be removed.

A cat may look at a king. I've read that in some book, but I don't remember where.

My dear! I wish you would have this cat removed!

Off with his head!

I'll fetch the executioner myself.

Alice thought she might well go back, and see ho the game was going on

Let's get on with the game.

Alice was too frightened to say a word, but followed the Queen back to the croquet ground.

Off with his head! Off with her head!

Those whom she sentenced were taken into custody by the soldiers, who of course had to stop being arches to do this.

By the end of half an hour or so, there were no arches left...

...and all the players, except the King, the Queen and Alice, were in custody and under sentence of execution.

Have you seen the Mock Turtle yet?

No, I don't even know what a Mock Turtle is.

It's the thing Mock Turtle Soup is made from.

I never saw one, or heard of one.

Come on, then, and he shall tell you his history.

You are all pardoned.

Alice had never been in a court of justice before, but she had read about them in books.

That's the judge because of his great wig. And that's the jury box. And those twelve creatures, I suppose they are the jurors.

She said this last word two or three times over to herself, being rather proud of it...

...for she thought, and rightly too, that very few little girls of her age knew the meaning of it at all.

What are they all doing? They can't have anything to put down yet, before the trial's begun.

They're putting down their names for fear they should forget them before the end of the trial.

Stupid things!

Silence in the court!

The guinea pig that cheered was immediately suppressed by the officers of the court.

I'm glad I've seen that done. I've so often read in the newspapers, at the end of trials...

'There was some attempt at applause, which was immediately suppressed by the officers of the court.'

And I never understood what it meant till now.

If that's all you know about it, you may stand down.

I can't go any lower. I'm on the floor, as it is.

Then you may go.

And the Hatter hurriedly left the court, without even waiting to put his shoes on.

Just take his head off outside.

But the Hatter was out of sight before the officer could get to the door.

The next witness was the Duchess's cook.

Call the next witness!

Give your evidence.

Shan't.

Your Majesty must cross-examine this witness.

Well, if I must, I must. What are tarts made of?

Pepper, mostly.

Treacle.

Treacle.

Collar that Dormouse! Behead that Dormouse! Turn that Dormouse out of court! Suppress him! Pinch him! Off with his whiskers!

For some minutes, the whole court was in confusion, getting the Dormouse turned out...

Call the next witness.

Really, my dear, you must cross-examine the next witness. It quite makes my forehead ache!

Alice!

...and by the time they had settled down again, the cook had disappeared.

Silence! Rule Forty-two. All persons more than a mile high to leave the court.

I'm not a mile high.

You are.

Nearly two miles high.

Well, I shan't go, at any rate. Besides, that's not a regular rule – you invented it just now.

It's the oldest rule in the book.

Then it ought to be Number One.

Consider your verdict.

There's more evidence to come yet, please your Majesty. This paper has just been picked up.

What's in it?

It must have been to somebody, unless it was written to nobody, which isn't usual.

It seems to be a letter, written by the prisoner to... to somebody.

But it isn't addressed to anyone. In fact, there's nothing written on the outside. It isn't a letter, after all. It's...

Wake up, Alice dear! Why, what a long sleep you've had!

Oh, I've had such a curious dream!

And she told her sister, as well as she could remember, all about the strange adventures she'd had.

It was a curious dream, dear, certainly. But now run in to your tea – it's getting late.

So Alice got up and ran off, thinking while she ran what a wonderful dream it had been.

But her sister sat still, thinking of little Alice and all her wonderful adventures...

...till she too began dreaming after a fashion.

And the whole place around her became alive with the strange creatures of her little sister's dream.

The long grass rustled at her feet, as the White Rabbit hurried by; the frightened Mouse splashed his way through the neighbouring pool...

...and she could hear the rattle of the teacups as the March Hare and his friends shared their never-ending mea

So she sat on, with closed eyes, and half believed herself in Wonderland.

Though she knew she only had to open them again, and all would change to dull reality.

The grass would only be rustling in the wind, and the pool rippling to the waving of the reeds.

The rattling teacups would change to tinkling sheep's bells...

BAA BAA

...the Queen's shrill cries to the voice of the shepherd boy...

...and the sneeze of the baby, the shriek of the Gryphon, and all the other queer noises, would change to the confused clamour of the busy farmyard...

...while the lowing of the cattle in the distance would take the place of the Mock Turtle's heavy sobs.

Lastly, she pictured how this same little sister of hers would, in later years, herself become a grown woman.

And how she would keep, through all her riper years, the simple and loving heart of her childhood.

And how she would gather other little children around her, and make their eyes bright and eager with many a strange tale.

Perhaps even with the dream of Wonderland of long ago.

And how she would feel with all their simple sorrows, and find a pleasure in all their simple joys...

...remembering her own childho and the happy summer days

About Us

It is night-time in the forest. The sky is black, studded with countless stars. A campfire is crackling, and the storytelling has begun. Stories about love and wisdom, conflict and power, dreams and identity, courage and adventure, survival against all odds, and hope against all hope — they have all come to the fore in a stream of words, gestures, song and dance. The warm, cheerful radiance of the campfire has awoken the storyteller in all those present. Even the trees and the earth and the animals of the forest seem to have fallen silent, captivated, bewitched.

Inspired by this enduring relationship between a campfire and the stories it evokes, we began publishing under the Campfire imprint in 2008, with the vision of creating graphic novels of the finest quality to entertain and educate our readers. Our writers, editors, artists and colourists share a deep passion for good stories and the art of storytelling, so our books are well researched, beautifully illustrated and wonderfully written to create a most enjoyable reading experience.

Our graphic novels are presently being published in four exciting categories. The *Classics* category showcases popular and timeless literature, which has been faithfully adapted for today's readers. While these adaptations retain the flavour of the era, they encourage our readers to delve into the literary world with the aid of authentic graphics and simplified language. Titles in the *Originals* category feature imaginative new characters and intriguing plots, and will be highly anticipated and appreciated by lovers of fiction. Our *Mythology* titles tap into the vast library of epics, myths, and legends from India and abroad, not just presenting tales from time immemorial, but also addressing their modern-day relevance. And our *Biography* titles explore the life and times of eminent personalities from around the world, in a manner that is both inspirational and personal.

Crafted by a new generation of talented artists and writers, all our graphic novels boast cutting-edge artwork, an engaging narrative, and have universal and lasting appeal.

Whether you are an avid reader or an occasional one, we hope you will gather around our campfire and let us draw you into our fascinating world of storytelling.

THE MYTHICAL and THE MAGICAL

GRIFFINS

Griffins are very strange creatures that have the body of a lion and the head and wings of an eagle. As we all know, the lion is the king of the beasts, and the eagle the king of the birds, so griffins are thought to be really powerful and majestic beasts. They live high in the mountains, make nests of gold, and lay precious stones instead of eggs. Ancient tales tell of the Arimaspians, the one-eyed race of Scythia, being great enemies of the griffins because they constantly tried to steal the treasure the griffins guarded.

In Alice in Wonderland, we see the Queen of Hearts ordering a griffin (spelt 'gryphon') to take Alice to see the Mock Turtle and hear its story.

PHOENIX

The most magnificent of all legendary birds, the red and golden phoenix is a symbol of immortality. According to Greek folklore, this beautiful bird lives near a well in Arabia and sings such a haunting song, that even the Sun stops to listen! It is said that it can live for up to a thousand years, and can even heal itself if injured. The phoenix never dies, so when it reaches the end of its lifespan, it builds itself a nest of spices and sets the nest, and itself, on fire. The phoenix then rises from the ashes and begins a new life.

In the book, *Harry Potter and the Chamber of Secrets*, Harry is wounded by a basilisk's fang and nearly dies from the venom. But Fawkes, a phoenix, heals the wound with his tears which have magic powers!

FAIRIES

These tiny magical creatures look like little humans with wings. It is said that fairies don't like to be seen by people at all and can appear and disappear in the blink of an eye. Supposedly there are bad fairies as well as good. Good fairies live among flowers and help humans, while bad ones steal babies. If you want fairies to visit your garden, you can leave a tiny piece of cake or biscuit for them. And, if you're lucky, you might see them dancing around rings of mushrooms in the moonlight. These are called fairy circles, which are believed to be the gateways to fairylands.

Tinker Bell, from the book *Peter Pan*, was a fairy who was good and kind to Peter in the island of Neverland. Her voice sounded like a tinkling bell and could be understood only by those who knew fairy language!

UNICORNS

Unicorns were enchanting creatures. They looked like white horses with a spiralling horn on their forehead. In the west, they were considered wild, while in the east they were gentle and thought to be bringers of good luck. In medieval folklore, the horn of the unicorns was called the alicorn, and was apparently magical. If it was dipped in dirty water, the water would become clean. Legend has it that when Noah gathered two of every kind of animal for his ark, he forgot to gather the unicorns, which is why they do not exist today. It is also said that unicorns are possibly based on the narwhal, a real-life sea creature with one horn.

In the fantasy novel series, *The Chronicles of Narnia* by CS Lewis, Jewel, the Unicorn, saves the life of Tirian, the last King of Narnia, in battle.

MORE MAGICAL MONSTERS

★ Centaurs were half man and half horse. Achilles, the Greek hero, had a teacher called Chiron who was a centaur.
★ The Yeti is a huge ape-like beast that lives in the foothills of the Himalayan mountains.
★ Leprechauns are imaginary creatures who live in Ireland and are found sitting on pots of gold.
★ Dragons are seen as fearsome creatures, but the Chinese believe they are good and friendly.

GOBLINS

Goblins are imaginary evil and mischievous creatures with long, pointed ears. And, do you know what they like doing? They love to rearrange household items, tangle up horses, bang pots and pans, and knock on doors and walls. Some even dig up graves and scatter the bones around! Goblins also like to stay in mines where they search for treasure. These magical creatures, though usually seen as troublemakers, are not completely evil. They like troubling the miserly and the lazy, and turn their rooms and things upside-down to teach them a lesson.

One of the earliest fairytales, *The Goblin and the Grocer* is a story about a goblin who has to choose between jam and poetry. In the end, he realises that though he thinks poetry is greater, he cannot give up the jam that he gets from the grocer!